THINK OF THINKING

RICARDO BERNAL

Hopeful Media
Solutions

ISBN 978-1-947920-05-7

Cover and interior design by Ashley Clarke at All Stories Editing

Published by Hopeful Media Solutions

845 East Highway 88

Suite 247

Jackson, CA 95642

www.HopefulMediaSolutions.com

*I dedicate this book to my parents, my awesome sister, **Sujey**, and her husband, Mike. This book is also dedicated to my loving brother, **Christobal**, and my beautiful daughter, **Skylynn**. And to everybody who understands me, thank you.*

DISCLAIMER

The information contained within this book is strictly for educational purposes. If you wish to apply ideas contained in this book, you are taking full responsibility for your actions.

FOREWORD

M.D. WHITE

Growing up in poverty without a father and watching my mother struggle to barely get by forced me to take on the entrepreneurial spirit and engage in business transactions as a minor. I started building and programing computers at the age of 8. Shortly thereafter, I was reselling hardware and software that I picked up from computer shows and big box stores. Unofficially and without a business license, I was operating a full service computer repair business. It seemed I was quickly becoming a success.

By the age of 18, I owned a very lucrative real estate port-folio, including several single family dwellings—one paid off entirely—and a small apartment complex, and a few small businesses. I was working night and day, nonstop, but I couldn't get to where I felt I was supposed to be: a self-made millionaire. On my 20th birthday, I was given a framed message, written by **James Lane Allen**, that transformed my life: "Man's rise or fall, success or failure, happiness or unhappiness, depends on his attitude... A man's attitude will create the situation he imagines."

The angel who blessed me with this framed message

suggested that I look into Napoleon Hill as well. I did. And the knowledge I obtained from these two individuals has been surpassed by none. In fact, with this newfound knowledge, I became a **multimillionaire** only days before my 21ˢᵗ birthday. It was that powerful. My life was forever changed.

When I met Ricardo, it was like a breath of fresh air. It was obvious that he was different from his peers... different from most. He had a great attitude, wonderful personality, and was always smiling and happy. It was clear that he was healthy, very much in shape, and had a great head on his shoulders. He wanted for nothing *but* to share a wonderful secret that changed his life. I listened intently, and to my amazement, I learned he studied from the same masters that changed my life. It was now clear why he had caught my attention immediately. We 'attracted' each other into our lives, a concept revealed in this book.

It was clear from our talks that Ricardo had a gift, by way of reducing volumes by various 'thought' masters in a clear, concise, coherent, and practical way, without losing any of the information that allowed the magic to work. So I challenged him to share his message with the world.

In a time when all have the desire for positive change but lack the time to research it enough to affect such change, Ricardo has provided the answer: *THINK OF THINKING*. This raw, uncut work provides all you need to change your life in the greatest way imaginable. There is truly no limit as to what the teachings of this book can bring you.

It has been my honor to be a part of this historical work, and to share with you what it has done for me.

—M.D.WHITE, #1 BESTSELLING AUTHOR OF *THE INFLUENCE OF MILITARY STRATEGIES TO BUSINESS*

INTRODUCTION

This great wisdom has transformed my life. My body, as well, has transformed at age 41. With this wisdom, I have befriended successful men and women that know about the truth of the power of the mind. I have great health, which creates strong energy that people recognize. I am relentless at making things happen. Because of this incredible wisdom, I am in a place many wish to be. I am seen as an asset in my work environment because of my mind-set.

I enjoy helping others, including my best friend at her job, keeping things in order to ensure success. Many people see and admire my way of being. I attract people with good energy, good circumstances, health, money, happiness, and strength with this knowledge. My life is what I always wanted it to be. I am my own master key to every door I desire to open. Any road I choose to travel on and any direction will be the right choice. Everything I touch will be blessed, because I have been blessed with this wisdom. This wisdom brings out the real me. I am thankful and happy with all my accomplishments. I am energized because everything I want, need, and wish for has always manifested.

My greatest achievement is helping others achieve all that they desire. Helping others gain what they desire and deserve is a huge goal in my life, one that I take seriously and execute with each breathe I take. I'm of the mindset that if *I* am doing it, I know you can do it as well. *Think of Thinking* is the start of a new life, a new way of thinking, and a way of recognizing who we, as humans, truly are. The power of our mind is real, so let's begin now.

THINK OF THINKING

If you're reading this right now, it's because you've attracted it into your life. Let me begin by telling you that my life has changed in the best way ever. All my life I've felt something within myself, something that has now been revealed to me in a special way. The situation I was in at the time this awakening became real was prison. Yes, prison is where I was given the truth about my way of thinking. I was on my bunk bed in my cell in the county jail when a dictionary was given to me. When I picked it up and opened it, the first word I saw was "arcane."

If you look up this word, it explains that only a few will be able to understand a certain special knowledge. This knowledge is now given to you. That's why I said that you yourself have attracted this incredible wisdom into your life. Have you ever been thinking about a song on the radio and seconds later, it plays? Well, you yourself have made it play on the radio by thinking of it. I understand that it sounds crazy, and that it was just coincidence. With this topic, only someone with the same mindset will be open minded and ready for the truth, because seeking is what got me here with you now. So my question to you is *What do you desire or want in your life?*

Nothing is created unless it's thought of first. Think about it. Cars that travel the world, in many different parts of different countries, were thought of first in the mind. The creator of the automobile had to think of it. He gave all his focus to what he wanted, and it became a reality.

This information was meant for you because you're ready for it now. Whatever you want in life, big or small, remember this: the more thought you put in to it, the stronger it becomes. Thinking of what you truly desire will place you in a positive position for the reality to manifest. When you think over and over and desire something with all your might, you tap into the unseen strong universal force. Once you tap in, things line up and set up to bring you the desire. The universe will influence people, situations, and conditions to pull all and everything you truly desire to you.

Before moving on, here is the Golden Rule: Never doubt. If you start to think negative, remind yourself, or better yet, know that what you're thinking and desiring will become reality by law.

We are all part of this incredible universe. We're only one component that makes up the universe, which gives us the master key to open any door we choose. This universal force has always been all around us. This is a small example. You have a television that's not plugged in. Your desire is to watch it, so you tell yourself, "I'll plug in the power," and then you turn it on. Once you plug in, you'll get the picture clearly. This force is here, we just need to plug into it to get its power so it can help us see the vision in our minds. This force is the main source that we must plug into to receive all we desire.

To really make things come to you faster and stronger, envisioning is the best way to pull all you desire toward you. Consider yourself a magnet. Close your eyes, and open your mind's eye, and cause things to happen. This universe is always on and ready to help, 24/7. When you're envisioning, you're thinking, and when you're seeing it, feeling it, living it in your mind, this great force responds and begins its process to pull things into your life. It's something super-difficult to try to understand. Our focus is not on figuring how it works, but knowing it's real and ready for us at all times. Notice that I keep repeating over and over how important it is to know that your thinking can bring or cause things to become real.

Repeating it many times to you is my goal, because your subconscious will download it into your brain. Also, I'm letting the brain know that it is time to create the life you desire.

I remember not having anything in life, being upset that everyone else had it all...except me. I would think, *Why don't I have enough money to make my life stress-free?* or *Why don't I have that nice home?* Well, I now know why. It was because I was thinking of what I didn't have instead of what I wanted. By changing my way of thinking from not having to wanting, the process of the universe began.

You can change situations by just changing your thinking. You deserve the finest things in life. Why stay in the same place? It's time to move forward and have your dreams become real. See yourself in that nice car, or see yourself in that beautiful home, or see yourself at the bank taking enough money out to live stress-free.

Everything you desire, you can have. Just envision yourself having it. Tap into this incredible universal force and see your life change. Be that strong magnet! Pull great opportunities into your life. Remember, you yourself attracted this real knowledge into your life. It's time to paint your awesome life with the paintbrushes you've received. The best way to define your future is by creating it yourself. You're the architect of your life, so build without any limits. The only limits you have are the ones you place in your life.

Open up your wings, and fly high above your past life, into the new, incredible life you deserve. If anyone tells you that it will never happen, run the opposite direction from them. Because everything is possible if you really think about it. They say that you can do anything if you put your mind to it. Close your eyes and your mind's eye, and think of what you truly desire.

You are what you think of most, so think success.

I truly hope that you'll find much greatness in your life. This is just the beginning of your new life. This information could have kept going into a huge book, but what is here will help you navigate in the right direction. This is your starting point. Good Luck!

WARNING: This knowledge is real, so please be careful. You cause negative situations that can bring sorrow. Think of it like having a rifle. You can use it to hunt game, to feed your family, protect your family, or the opposite thereof. Thank you for thinking.

—*Ricardo Bernal*

ACKNOWLEDGMENTS

Before moving forward, thank you, M.D White. I'm inspired by your kindness and wisdom. Without your incredible support, this book would have not been created. I also thank Hopeful Media Solutions for the opportunity you have given me.

To my beautiful, loving parents, thank you for showing me unconditional love and understanding. To my brother **Christobal**—words can't express the love I feel for you. To my awesome sister **Sujey**, you're the strongest woman I've ever known. I love you, **Niña**. To your husband, Mike, thank you for all your support. To my daughter **Skylynn**, you're the heartbeats of my heart.

I thank all my friends and teachers that believed in me —thank you. To my cousins, Jorge and Nena, thank you for all the love and respect you send me.

To all the seekers of truth, the dreamers, stay focused, move forward, and be happy. Thank you!

I would like to acknowledge all the men and women around the world that motivated me to start my journey. Many things in life, positive or negative situations, can create good or bad opportunities. Since my life was always a crazy ride, I decided to convert it into a golden opportunity. I started to seek and ask questions about truth. Books of great wisdom came to me, and soon after, people with the same mindset begin to wake me up. The connection we had was incredible. Many keys were given to me.

So with much joy, I truly thank all my friends. **Napoleon Hill**, **Charles F Haaney**, **Genevieve Mulford**, **Wallace Wattles**, and all the great thinkers of yesterday, today, and tomorrow....

ABOUT THE AUTHOR

RICARDO BERNAL is a self-described humanitarian who has overcome the complexities of life, and has now dedicated his life—and new found knowledge—to helping others. He prides himself as an up and coming GURU of the "New Thought" Movement, with an emphasis on his 'message' and **NOT** on the publicity of giving it. He has selflessly motivated, helped, inspired, and assisted all those around him, and those who have crossed his path have now set out, with purpose, to transform the world with his message of guaranteed health, happiness, and success for all who wish to have it. He currently resides in Ione, California.

Learn more by visiting:

www.HopefulMediaSolutions.com

ORIGINAL MEDIA RELEASE

**THINK OF THINKING, the upcoming instant bestseller,
reveals the secret to guaranteed health, wealth, and prosperity.**

New Thought and motivational expert, Ricardo Bernal, has released his book, *Think of Thinking*, a new thought guide to life that takes the best practices and teaches you how you can apply them in your life, work, or business successfully. The book is scheduled for release on February 1st.

As a leader in the New Thought Movement, Ricardo Bernal wrote this book, which utilizes the teachings of the most sought-after experts from the last 2,000 years, coupled with his countless experiences over the years, to lay out working, tested, trusted, and simplified instructions for a guaranteed life full of great health, extraordinary wealth, and unbelievable happiness. Bernal had this to say: "You can have anything you mind can dream of, or your heart desires. I mean anything—this is real. There is no other amount of knowledge or wisdom that can prepare you better than the secrets you'll receive from this manual. It is truly life changing. I am living proof."

Many have deliberated over the various techniques espoused by past experts, but Ricardo Bernal cuts to the chase, simplifying their ideas for all, and reveals the raw secrets you need to learn. In this book, Bernal extracts the most important element, one that is left out in most discussions. For the first time ever, there is a clear, concise, and easy-to-understand roadmap to learning how to unlock your desired dreams.

The author further stressed the effectiveness of this life changing secret. "No matter how big or small your dreams are, you can have them. If you want perfect health, it's yours. If you wish to be rich, you will become rich. If you want a lifetime of prosperity, it is all with your grasp—and this manual is your ticket. You'll need nothing more."

MEDIA CONTACT

Company Name: Hopeful Media Solutions
    Contact Person: Rebecca Juarez, VP Public Relations
    URL: www.hopefulmediasolutions.com
    Phone: 209-781-5868
    Address: 845 East Highway 88, Suite 247 Jackson, CA 95642

HOSTILE INTENT: GAME ON

After two planes strike the World Trade Center, causing mass casualties and a wave of terror to crash over the nation, the United States faces a new threat, one it hasn't had to consider since the Civil War: the possibility of an attack from within its own shores. Which means it needs a plan.

Luckily, Patrick O'Malley already has one. With the support of the president and his specialized team behind him, O'Malley sets out to ensure that his country remains safe from terror attacks, wherever they may come from. And they are coming.

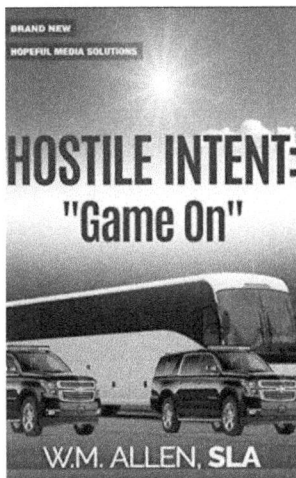

GEORGE'S GIRLS

George is living the good life. A high-ranking member of the executive trouble shooting team for Parks across the country, George spends his semi-retired life on the road in his custom Newell Coach, practically a studio apartment on wheels.

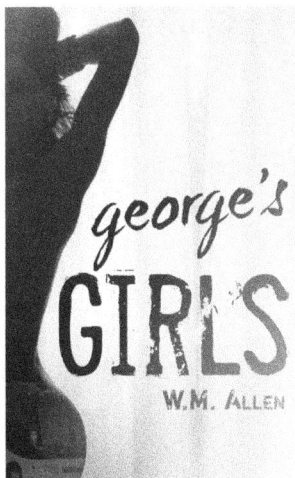

It's a nice, cushy job for an old man like him, not to mention his favorite perk—the women he meets along the way.

Because there's nothing George loves more than a young woman thirsty for attention. Amber, a drop-dead gorgeous clerk at the Pamp's general store, is exactly that, and she's dying for a taste of a real man.

It's not long before Amber, an exotic artist named Eve, and a collection of other women from across the Park come together for the erotic adventure of a lifetime.

George's Girls is a sensual roller coaster from start to finish, full of intrigue, drama, and enough heat to steam up even the most extravagant coach.

THE INFLUENCE OF MILITARY STRATEGIES TO BUSINESS

The world of business is a battlefield. You must be prepared.

Sun Tzu said, "The art of war teaches us to rely not on the likelihood of the enemy's not coming, but on our own readiness to receive him." The takeaway? Do everything in your power to be prepared, because it's only a matter of time before something goes wrong. If you are running, founding, working in any business, or are in an environment where 'politics' yield to nobody, The Influence of Military Strategies to Business is the preparation you need to succeed.

This military-based guide to business takes the best wartime tactics and practices and teaches you how you can apply them in your business—and your personal life—successfully. With its systematic and comprehensive framework, this book utilizes the art of war in a whole new way and reveals that the path to a smooth business victory can be found in an unexpected but rewarding place.

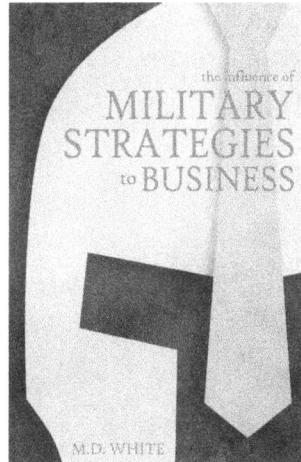

SOON TO COME BY RICARDO BERNAL

Thinking Is Power

Think of Health

Think of Money